RED

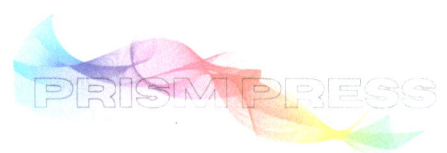

© 2025 Prism Press.
All rights reserved.
No part of this publication may be reproduced
without permission of the publisher.

IN ALPHABETICAL ORDER

REEM BASSOUS

MORGAN DANNER

MAHSA DEHGHAN

PIET MURA

PABLO NAVARRO-MACLOCHLAINN

ENNE TESSE

Red, other than black and white, was humanity's earliest color. As early as 75,000 years ago, people ground red ochre into powder to paint cave walls for rituals of survival, fertility, and reverence. From the beginning, red was not just a color but a symbol.

In Western traditions, red came to embody passion and intimacy, appearing in roses, love letters, and Valentine's Day rituals. It also carried the weight of danger and violence, the fiery hue of blood, flames, and warning signals. At the same time, red signified status and ceremony, from the crimson robes of cardinals and royal mantles to today's red carpet, a declaration of power and prestige. Universally, it functions as a warning color, commanding attention in stop signs, traffic lights, and emergency vehicles. Beyond caution, red channels excitement, energy, and aggression, making it a favored tool in branding and marketing. It signals power and dominance, whether in a businessman's "power tie" or the luxurious flow of a red carpet. In fashion, red projects wealth, confidence, and boldness, epitomized by the iconic red soles of Christian Louboutin shoes. And in the realm of appetite, it stimulates desire, frequently used in restaurant logos and food packaging to entice and allure.

Across cultures, red continued to embody meanings at once universal and contradictory. In Asia, red is an auspicious tones. In China it is the emblem of prosperity and happiness, central to weddings, festivals, and New Year celebrations. Red envelopes, or hongbao, promise luck and blessings. In Japan, the vermilion, an orangish-red, torii gates of Shinto shrines stand as guardians against evil.

In Tibet, red is also considered a sacred color particularly in Tibetan Buddhist practice. Red is used on the walls of sacred Buddhist temples to symbolize protection. Red is specifically linked to the Buddha Amitabha, the celestial Buddha, and meditating on the color is believed to help transform the delusion of attachment into the wisdom of discernment.

In India, red is sacred to marriage and fertility, worn in bridal saris, the part in the hair and a dot on the forehead, a mark symbolizing marital bond. In Hinduism, the color red holds deep symbolic meaning, representing auspiciousness, passion, power, and purity, particularly in the context of weddings and festivals.

Elsewhere, red carried different layers of meaning. In South Africa, red is a color of mourning, its presence in the national flag acknowledging bloodshed and struggle during apartheid. In ancient Egypt, red was dual-natured: a color of celebration and victory, yet also linked to danger, chaos, and the god Set, who ruled the desert.

In Russia, red is associated with life and passion. Red eggs are a traditional Russian Easter symbol representing Christ's resurrection and is also notably seen in Russian folk costumes. Additionally, red in Russia is famously associated with communism, symbolizing the blood of workers and prominently featured in Soviet symbolism. During the Soviet era, children were required to wear red scarves as members of a communist youth group.

In Arabia, red paradoxically symbolizes love, passion, caution and war. In modern Arab flags, red often represents the Hashemite dynasty and the bloodshed in the struggle for freedom. The Lebanese flag uses red to symbolize the blood of martyrs who fought against Ottoman rule, while in the Jordanian flag, it represents the reigning Hashemite dynasty.

In Persian culture, the color red holds significant and diverse symbolic meanings that are evident across various aspects of life and traditions. During celebrations and rituals, like Nowruz (the Persian New Year), red signifies joy, prosperity, and vitality. Red apples, in particular, symbolize health and happiness. In traditional Iranian clothing, the color red is frequently used and embodies different meanings depending on the specific region and its unique cultural and ethnic identity.

Among the Maya and Aztec people, red pigments drawn from cochineal insects and cinnabar were vital in ritual, symbolizing sacrifice, regeneration, and the sacred force of blood. Among many Native American peoples, red embodied war and success in battle but also the cycle of life and renewal.

The symbolism of red is deeply enmeshed with the history of art. In Rome, it colored walls and garments, a marker of wealth and dominance. By the Renaissance, red was the most precious pigment reserved for icons, illuminated manuscripts, and the portraits of nobility. Painters like Titian and Raphael used its depth to convey both sensuality and divine authority, while Caravaggio draped his scenes in crimson cloth to heighten drama and pathos. In modern and contemporary art, red became not only symbolic but also experiential. Henri Matisse's Harmony in Red(1908) envelops the viewer in a field of color, making red less a symbol than an environment. Mark

Rothko's vast canvases of layered reds turn color into a meditative force, inviting viewers into silence and transcendence. For Kazimir Malevich, Red Square (1915) embodied revolution, a radical break from tradition. Ai Weiwei has used red as both a sign of Chinese cultural identity and as a tool of critique against political power. From the red dress in van Eyck's Arnolfini Portrait to Christ's robe in El Greco's Disrobing of Christ, from Malevich's abstraction to Keith Haring's Red Radiant Baby, artists have continually returned to this primal pigment. Red is, at its core, a paradox. It sanctifies and profanes, protects and endangers, seduces and repels. That it was the first color our ancestors chose to paint with is no accident: red embodies the extremes of human existence, carrying within it both the lifeblood of survival and the fire of transcendence.

by Rula J. Brock

REEM BASSOUS

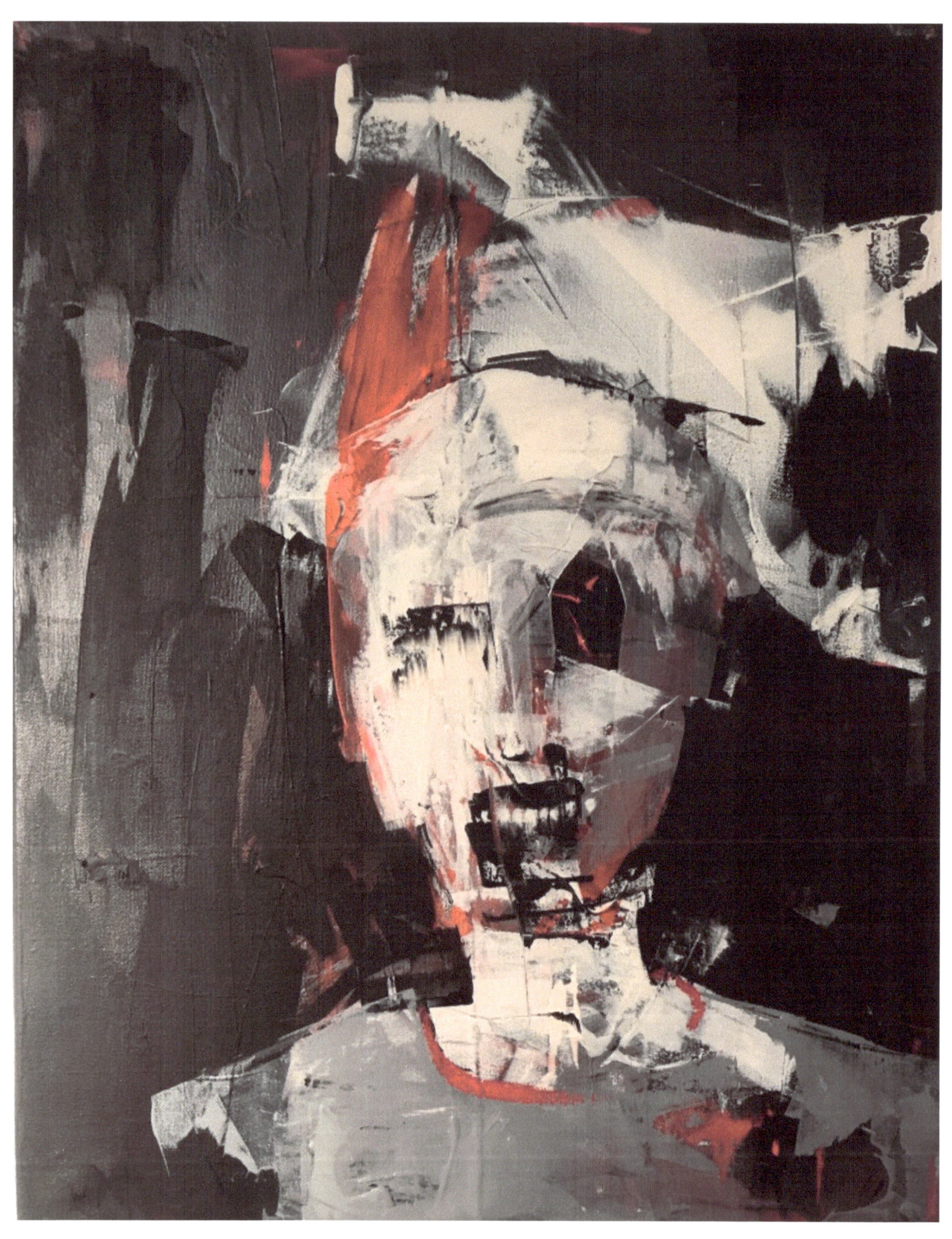

REEM BASSOUS, MORIBUND OUTLIVERS I

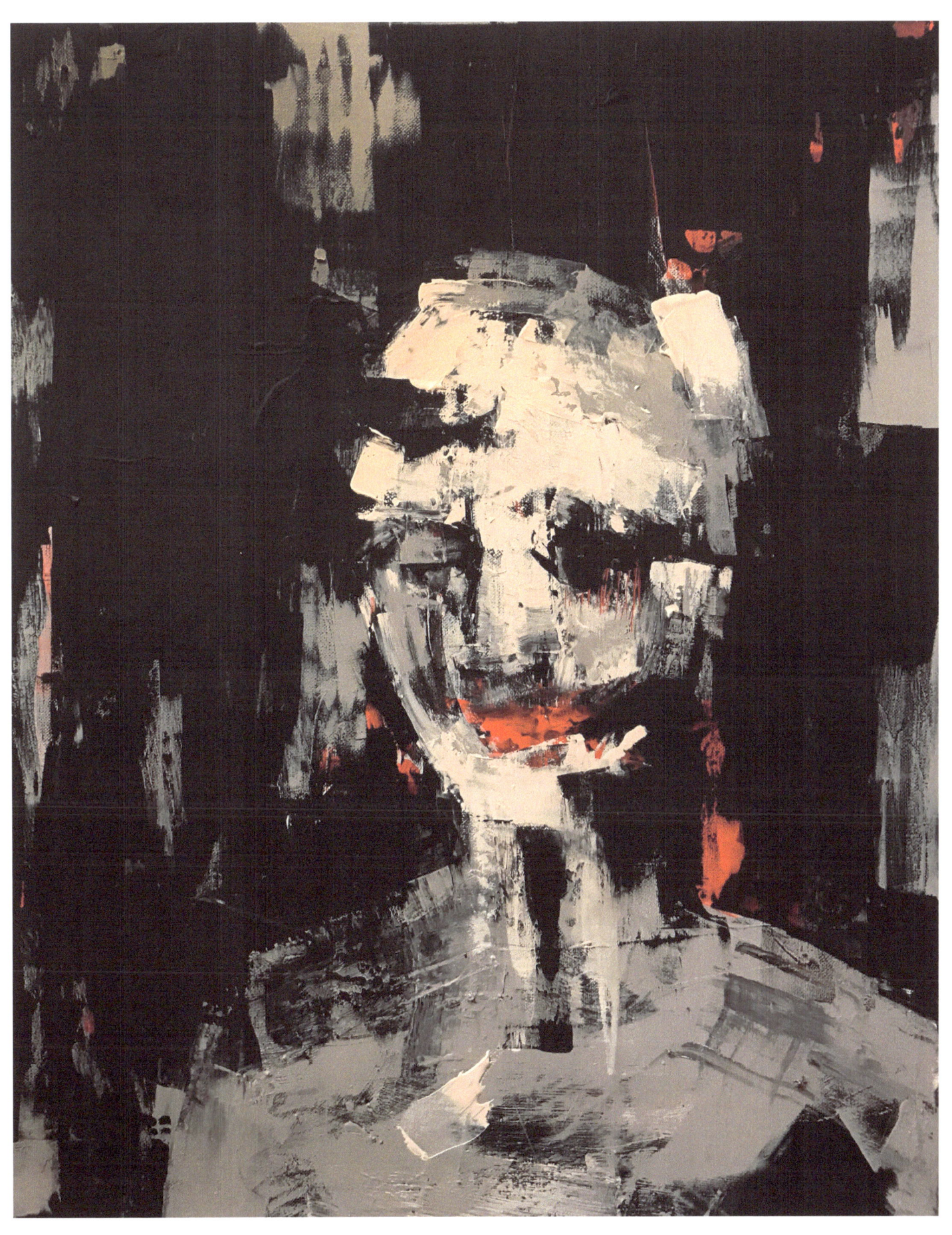

REEM BASSOUS, MORIBUND OUTLIVERS II

"No longer posthumous, the survivor is not an overliver who aimlessly questions the significance of his brute survival, but rather a witness who knows too much, carrying the weight of an unwelcome knowledge gathered from within war and crisis that challenges the official closure of the present to the unfinished past."

- Walid Sadek, Lebanese artist and writer

In her series *Moribund Outlivers*, Reem Bassous writes that "the postwar survivor appears in the form of a Moribund, someone who negotiates the path in between life and death." The figure in this work does not arrive through deliberate construction but through what Bassous calls the paint's own assault: *"These figures are not formed deliberately; the paint determines how they appear (or disappear). The paint delivers the assault which shapes these Moribunds in their habitats."*

The image bears this struggle in its fractured marks. Black masses swallow form while swathes of white blur recognition. Streaks of red punctuate the surface like wounds, signaling both vitality and violence. The face is not a face but a suggestion of one, a site of erasure as much as emergence. Red operates at once as wound, voice, and trace of life. Unlike the blacks and whites that dominate and obscure form, red insists. It cuts through the surface, punctuating the otherwise ashen palette with an intensity that feels both vital and violent.

Bassous echoes Gilles Deleuze's reading of Francis Bacon, where the philosopher described the *"hysteria of the mark"* as paint that resists calm representation and instead erupts into chaos and force. In Bassous' portraits, this frenzy of paint disrupts figuration, leaving us to ask, in her own words, *"What quantifies a figure? What quantifies a head without a face?"* These questions unsettle our assumptions about what makes a person recognizable, or even what makes them human in the aftermath of violence.

Survival, in this vision, is not a clean resolution or a triumphant recovery. Instead, it is the act of endurance, the body and the face holding together just enough to persist, yet always on the verge of dissolution. The Moribund lives suspended between recognition and disappearance, never fully one or the other.

This suspension becomes a haunting embodiment of postwar memory and its fragility. The paintings do not offer comfort or closure; they offer a raw confrontation with what it means to live on after catastrophe. In the streaks of red, the smears of white, and the swallowing black, we see not only the marks of trauma but also the fragile insistence of existence itself.

MORGAN DANNER

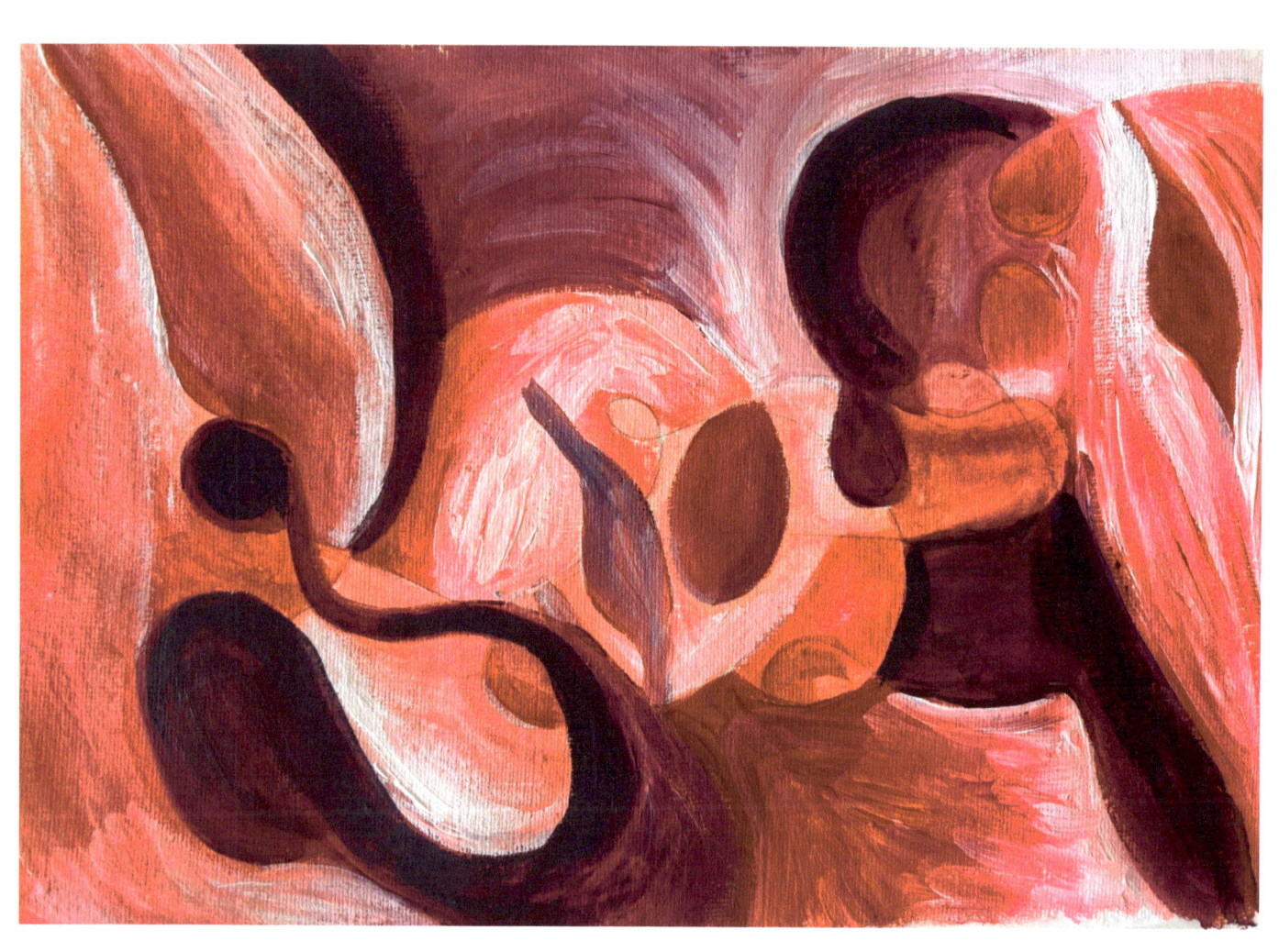

MORGAN DANNER, CRIMSON TERRAFORM

Crimson Terraform

The flag crumbled,
tossed like discarded old sheets.
Liberty was rebranded,
weaponized,
and fed to the faithful.
Now the land reshapes itself
—red, raw, and ruled by silence.

    -Morgan Danner

Morgan Danner, an American architect living in Italy, presents a non-objective painting that explore the expressive range of the color red. Rather than anchoring her compositions in recognizable forms, Danner allows red to become the subject itself, layered, shifting, and alive with variation.

In this work, reds fold and unfold upon themselves, creating undulating spaces that suggest multiple possibilities at once. They suggest landscapes glimpsed from above, cavernous interiors, or draped textiles in motion. The imagery resists resolution, hovering in the liminal space between abstraction and suggestion. By working across a spectrum of values, from deep maroon to luminous pink, Danner builds a visual terrain where depth, light, and shadow seem to pulse within the surface.

As an architect, her sensitivity to structure and space resonates through the paintings. The forms curve, overlap, and conceal, evoking the sensation of entering a place that is at once intimate and expansive. Never fully resolving into fixed identities, the works remain provisional, alive with ambiguity, leaving the viewer suspended in a state of continual becoming.

MAHSA DEHGHAN

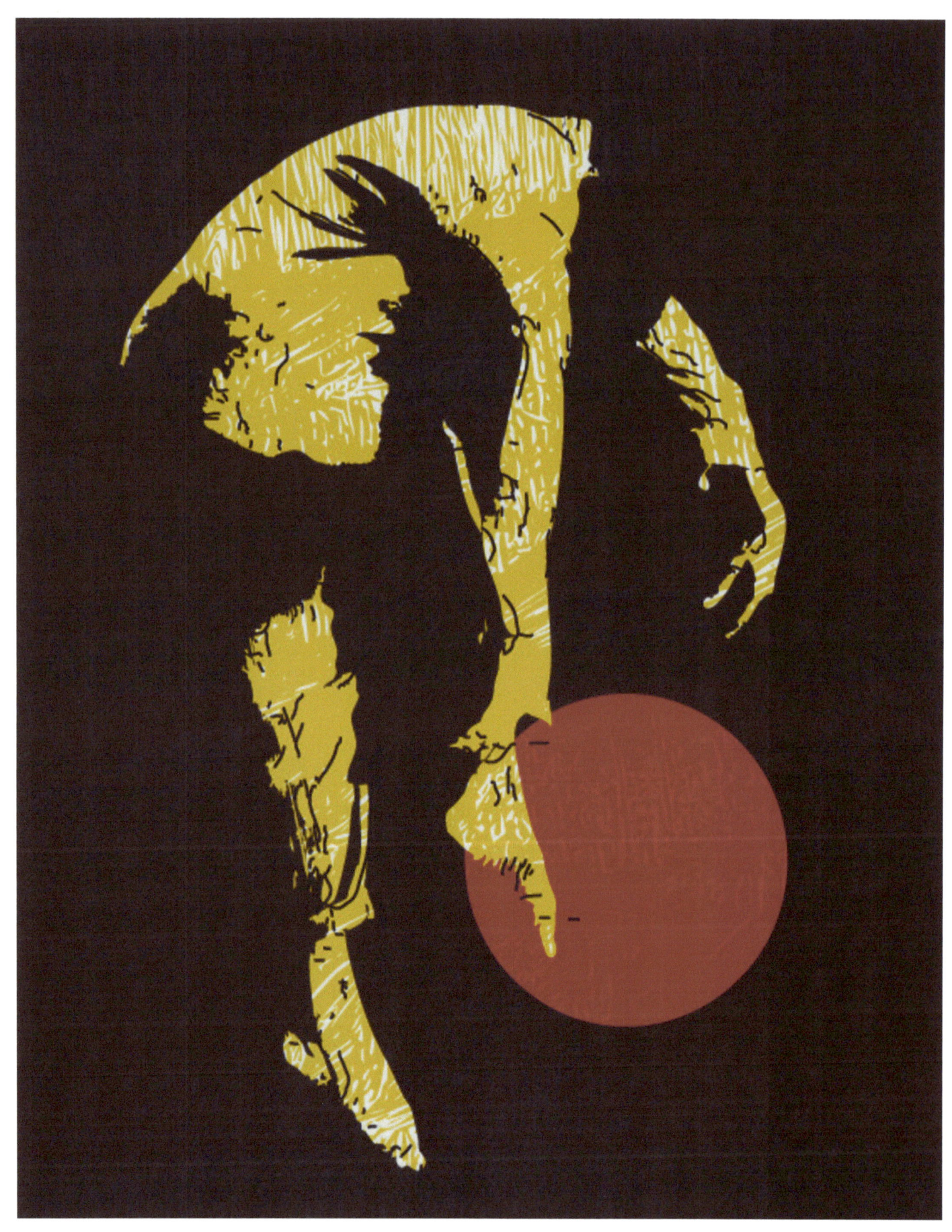

MAHSA DEHGHAN, CIRCLE OF EXISTENCE

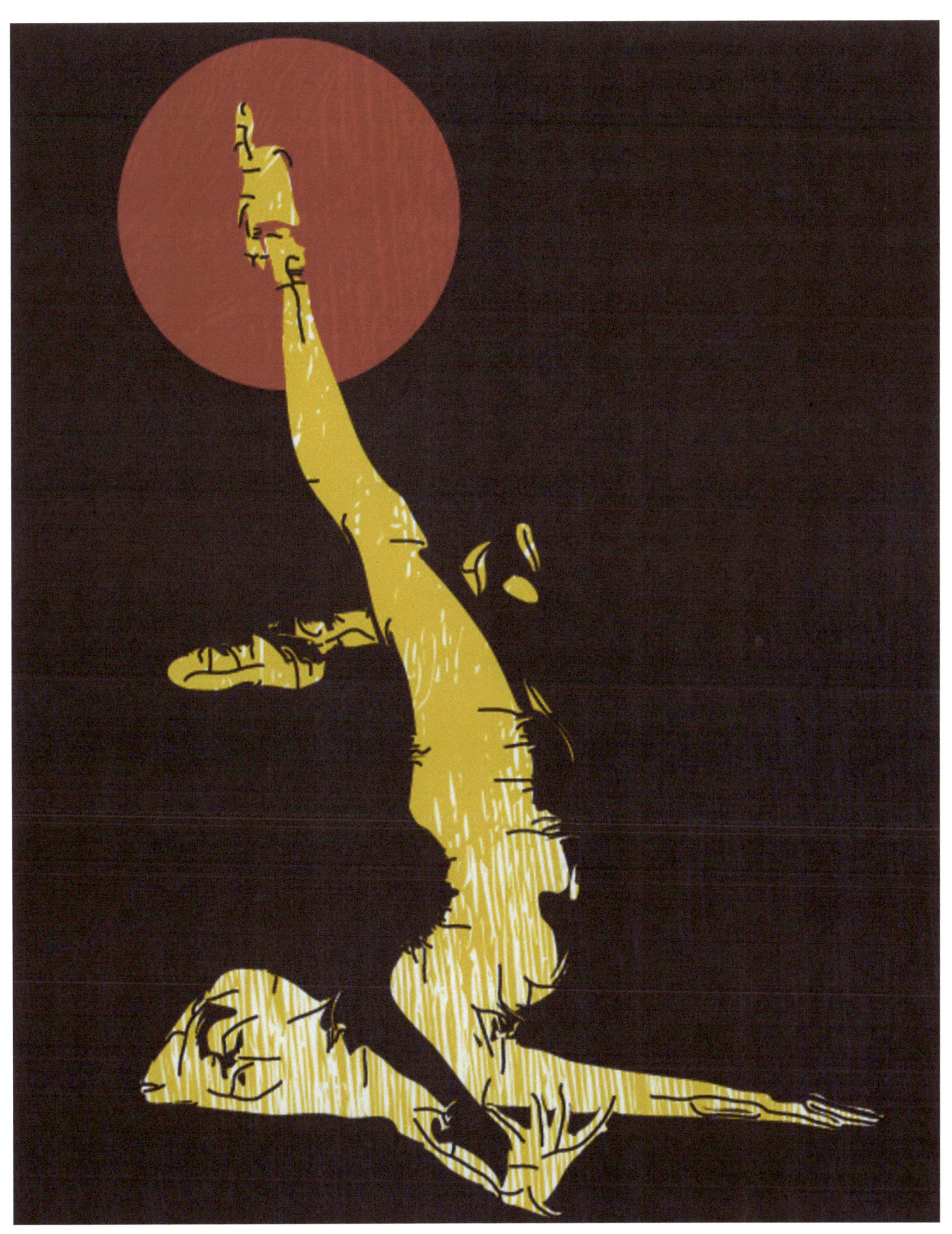

MAHSA DEHGHAN, CIRCLE OF EXISTENCE

"Life moves in cycles rather than straight lines. From birth to death we pass through stages that shape us, moments of joy, suffering, growth, loss, freedom and restraint. The circle of existence reminds us that each of these stages is connected, that endings are never final but instead give way to new beginnings.

Every person's journey within this circle is unique. We may see someone dancing in joy while inside they may be carrying unseen struggles, or we may witness suffering that hides untold strength. The circle holds all of these emotions at once, passion and despair, hope and fear, creation and collapse.

To recognize the circle of existence is to accept life's rhythm, an endless flow of transformation where no stage is permanent, and no experience can fully reveal the hidden depths of another's journey. It teaches humility, empathy, and the understanding that behind every human face lies a story we cannot fully know."

-Mahsa Dehghan

In these mixed media works, by Mahsa Dehghan, the red circle functions as a visual and symbolic anchor. Against the fractured textures of the golden human forms, red holds steady as the constant reminder of the cycle of life. It embodies the circle of existence that Mahsa Dehghan describes, birth, death, and renewal flowing into one another.

Red here does not waver between meanings but stands firmly as the emblem of the eternal cycle. It is the shared pulse behind every individual journey, the presence that reminds us that endings fold into beginnings, and that within the vast circle of existence, we are anchored to something larger than ourselves.

PABLO NAVARRO–MACLOCHLAINN

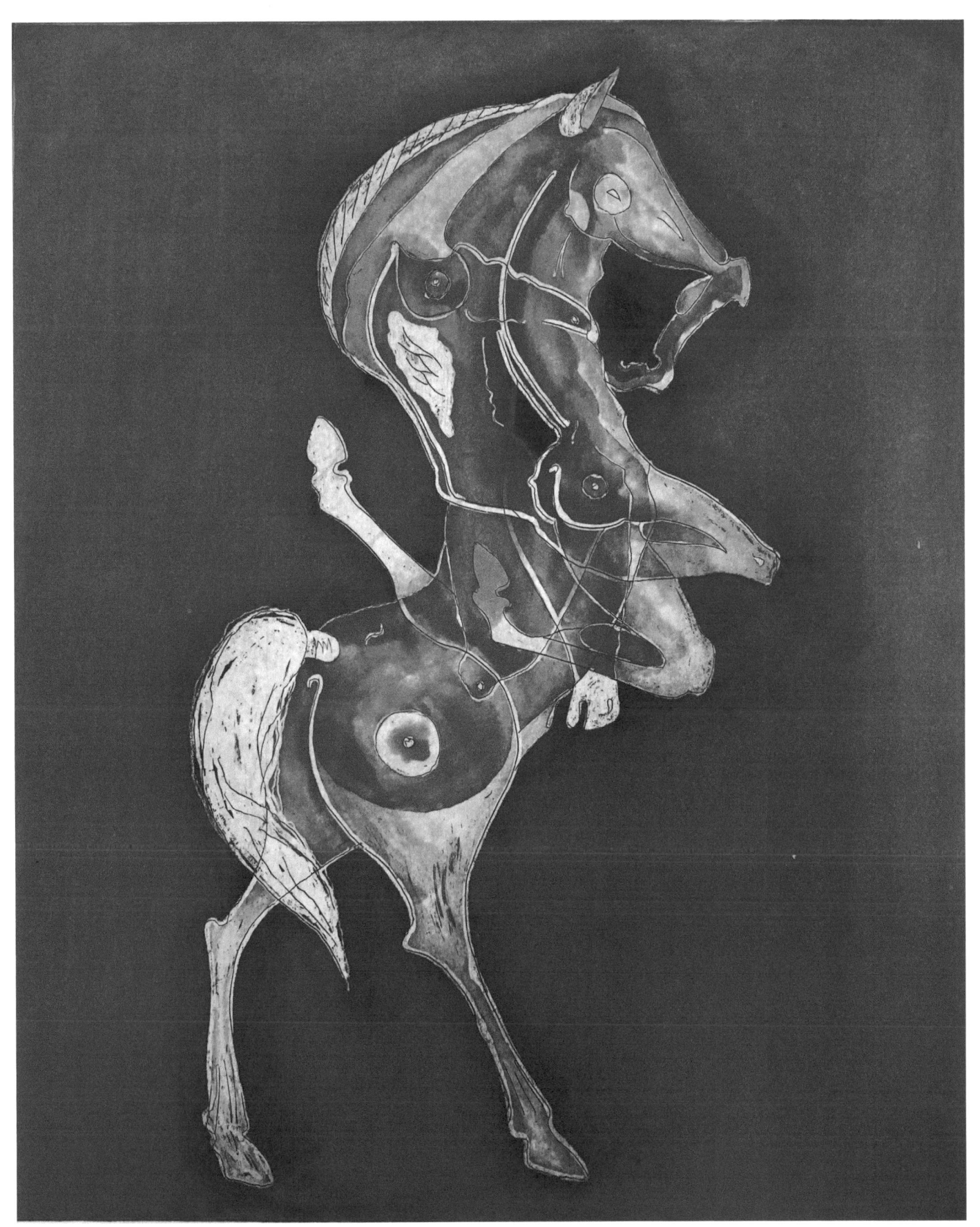

PABLO NAVARRO–MACLOCHLAINN
DIVA IS THE FEMALE VERSION OF A OSTLER

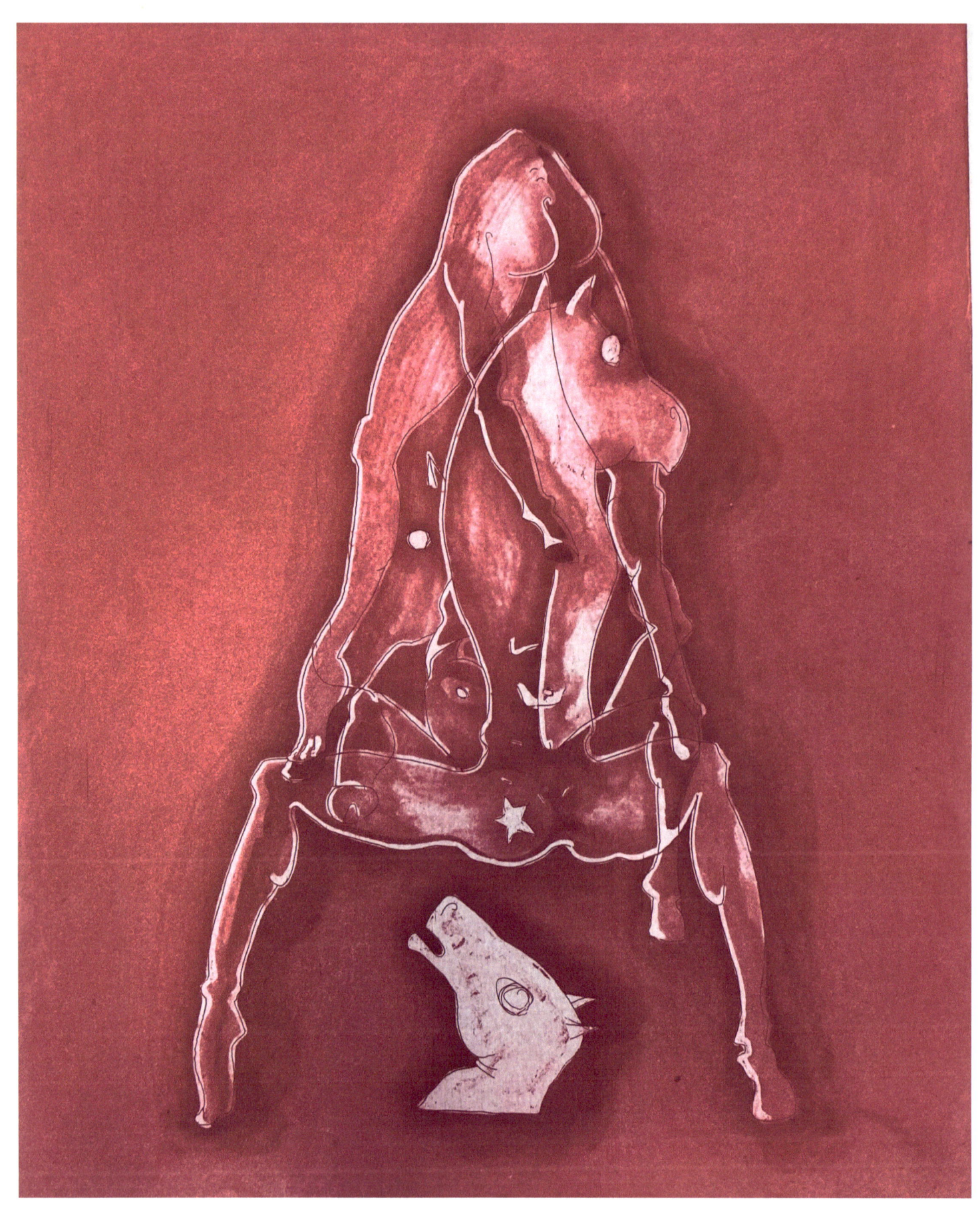

PABLO NAVARRO-MACLOCHLAINN

THIRSTY BOY

Pablo Navarro-MacLochlainn (British-Irish, b.1987) works with print and sound to explore notions of desire and disgust. Queering the traditional media of etching and aquatint with irreverent, Tumblr-coded imagery, he interfaces the sexy and the repulsive, provoking discomfort and a reexamination of the viewer's values. His recent series, Horsies, shown here, addresses the canon of equestrian art and the dubious legacy of illustrative Brony pornography, a scenic tour of the internet's red-light district.

In these works, red saturates the entire image field, transforming it into an animalistic zone where instinct reigns. It is the color of heat, flesh, and urgency.

Red functions as a chromatic skin that collapses distinctions between eroticism and creaturely instinct.

By flooding the surface in red, Navarro-MacLochlainn anchors the work in the body's raw immediacy. Red is an animalistic force that reminds us that beneath layers of culture, fetish, and digital remix, the body still insists, unfiltered and alive.

PIET MURA

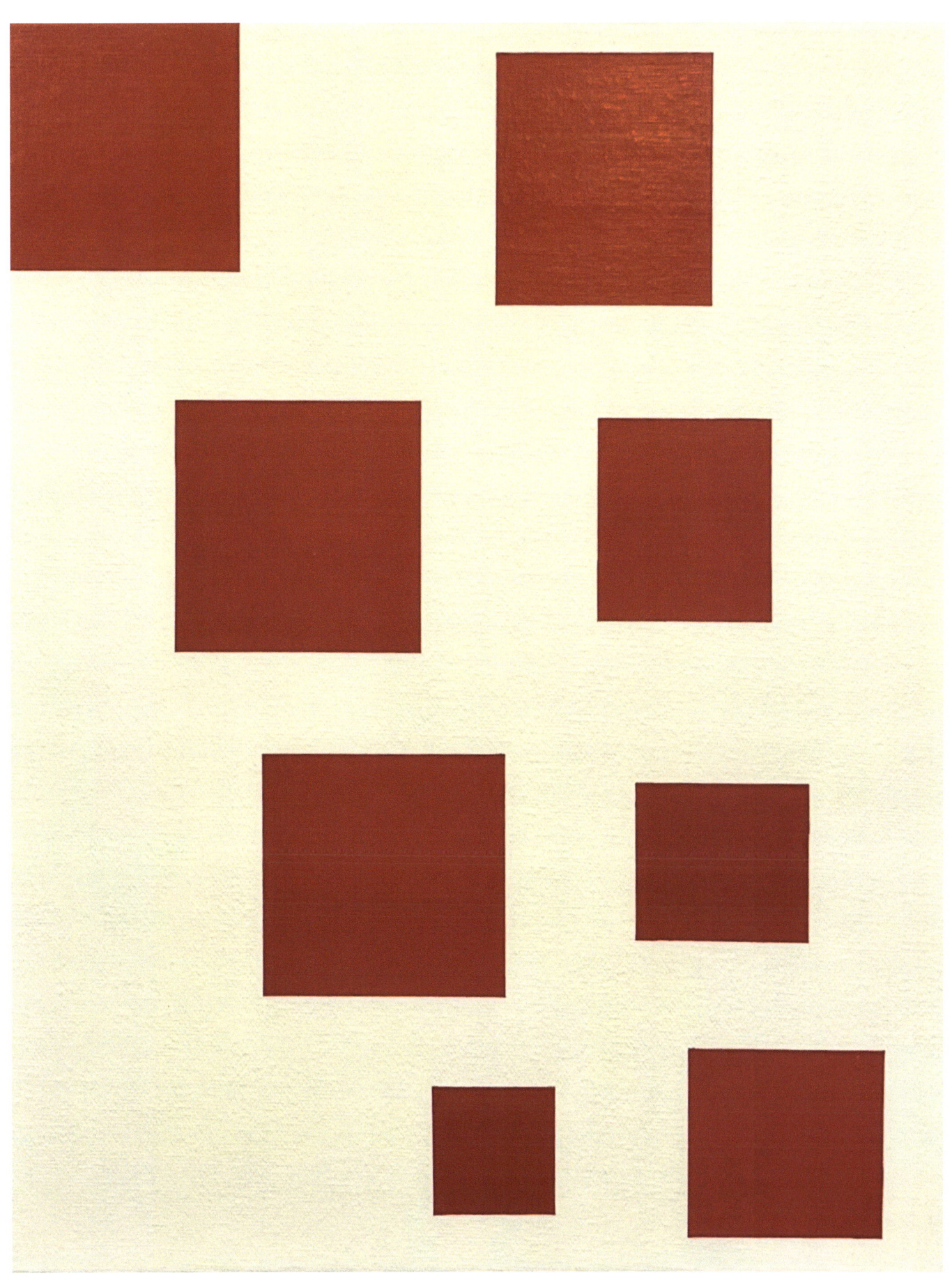

PIET MURA, ENVY

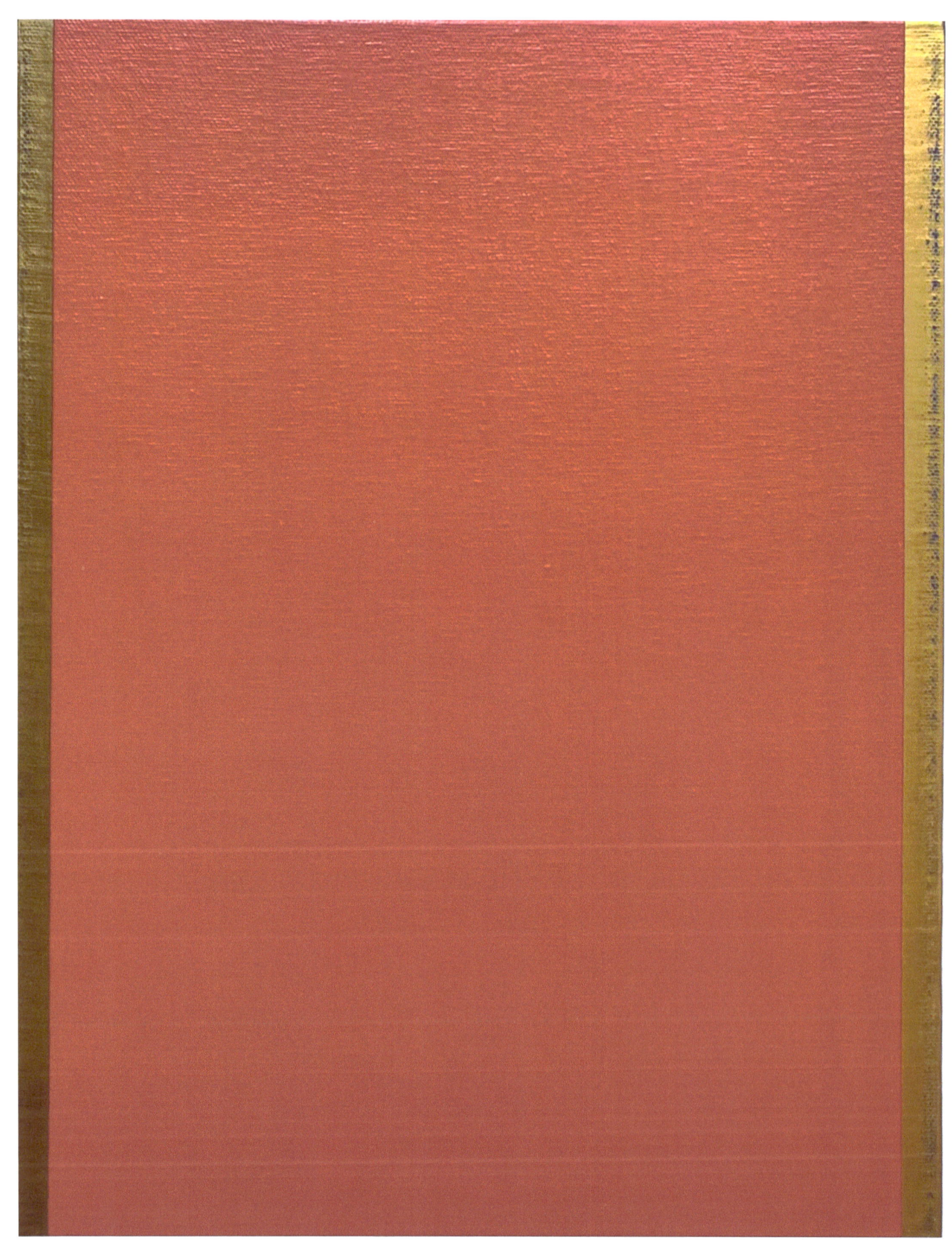

PIET MURA, IRA

"Red is power.
Red is energy.
Red is emotion."

-Pict Mura

To understand Piet Mura's work, one has to understand its conversation with art history. Mura is not painting "pictures" in a traditional sense, but responding to a century of artists who wrestled with the meaning of pure color and form.

In *Envy,* the floating red squares on a neutral background recall Piet Mondrian and the Dutch movement De Stijl, or "the style," which used strict grids and primary colors to express universal harmony. Mura loosens that order: his squares are scattered, less rigid, more open, turning Mondrian's rules into rhythm.

More over, *Envy* directly references Kazimir Malevich's Suprematist Composition with *Eight Red Rectangles* (1915), a landmark work in non-objective art. The title *Envy* acknowledges the impossibility of surpassing such a radical achievement, positioning Mura's own work as both homage and recognition of the limits of artistic ambition.

In *Ira*, Mura washes the surface with a single glowing red field bordered by gold, echoing Barnett Newman's monumental paintings of the 1960s. Newman believed color itself could be overwhelming and even spiritual, and his *Who's Afraid of Red, Yellow and Blue* series famously confronted audiences with that challenge. Mura's homage makes red both expansive and reverent, situating it as a color that still carries the weight of history, emotion, and presence.

ENNE TESSE

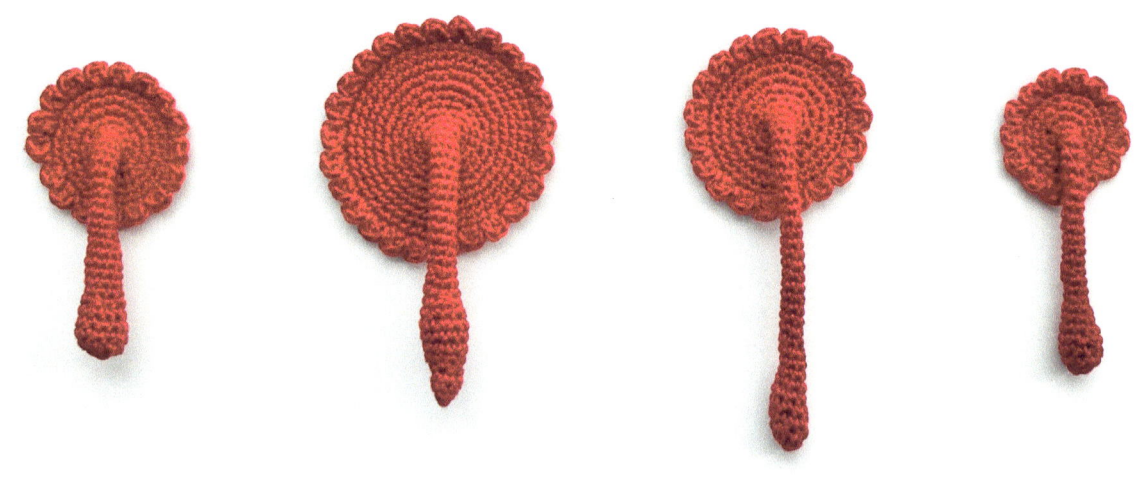

ENNE TESSE, QUARTETTO

*"The dripping sounds of red.
Do you hear us?
This is our sinfonietta."*
-Enne Tesse

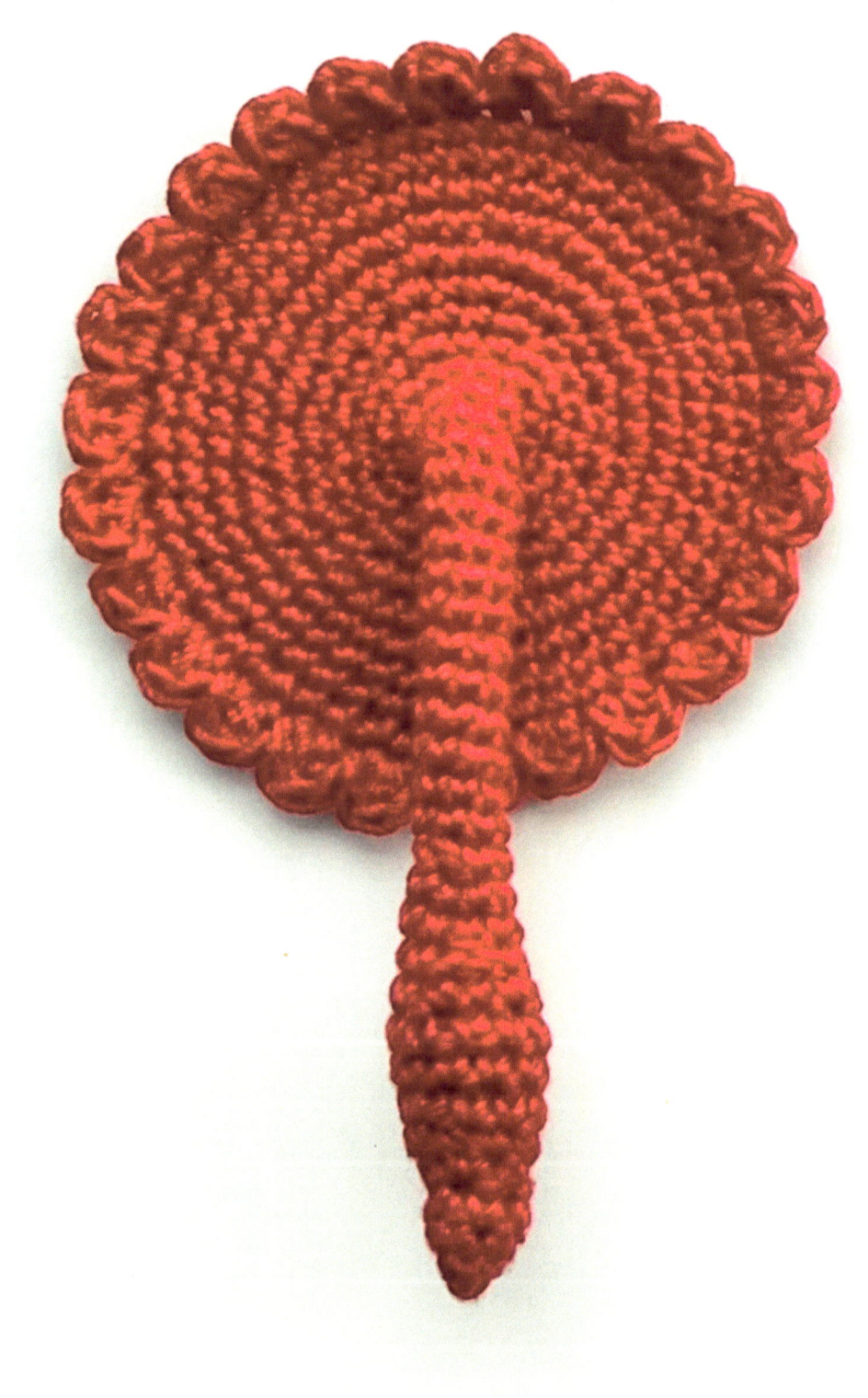

ENNE TESSE, QUARTETTO, DETAIL

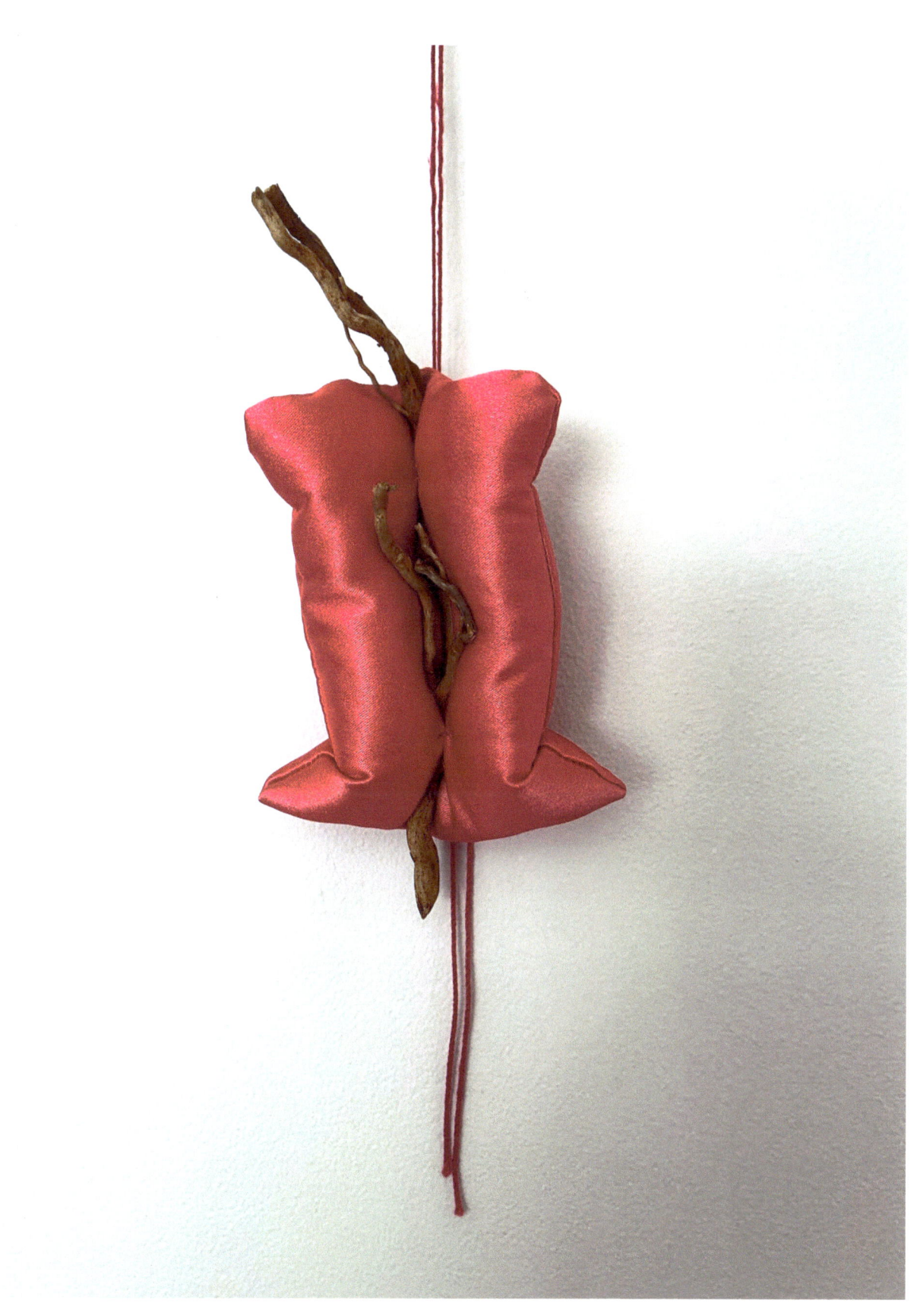

ENNE TESSE, HELD 2

"I view fabric and written words as layers that can offer modifications and transformations, simulate protection and provide concealment. I am interested in repetitive acts, rituals, patterns, rhythms, and the act of reading. I revisit and reimagine familiar objects while challenging the ways we perceive and interact with fabric and written words. Organs and body parts are concepts that inspire my work. I use textiles of natural and synthetic fibers including rope, cord and twine as well as component parts of used book pages. I produce my work through detailed and precise use of the hand. My creative process involves cutting, rearranging, sewing, and collaging. Visual and tactile components are linked in my work. My works generate from the transformative qualities of these functional materials."

-Enne Tesse

In both of these pieces, red becomes the binding force.

Quartetto consists of four crocheted red forms, circular with scalloped edges, each extending downward into a narrow, tapering "drip." Hung in sequence, they evoke both bodily organs and ritual objects, their repetition suggesting rhythm and duration. The choice of crochet, with its looping, accumulative structure, reinforces the sense of pulse and continuity, each stitch an act of counting, each form an echo. Red here becomes more than a color: it is an auditory image, a vibration. The installation becomes a "sinfonietta" or a small symphony, where each red form plays a part in a larger score of the body, the feminine, and the collective.

By linking fabric, rhythm, and the color red, Tesse turns crochet into testimony. Red is not static but active, dripping, speaking, sounding. It is both material and voice, a reminder that the body persists, resists, and resounds through ritual and repetition.

In Held 2, the satin-stuffed form pierced by a twisted branch, the material gleams like flesh, recalling both softness and exposure. Red here is protective yet vulnerable, a covering that cannot fully conceal the organic intrusion of wood. In the crocheted sequence of circular forms, red is multiplied through repetition, rhythm, and scale. The hand-worked surfaces evoke organs, flowers, or ritual medallions, blurring domestic craft with bodily presence.

Red in Tesse's practice is not decorative but corporeal. It intensifies the link between fabric and flesh, ritual and rhythm. Whether plush or crocheted, her red textiles pulse with the vitality of organs and the memory of touch, situating the body as both subject and material of transformation.

Works Cited:

Ames-Lewis, Francis. Drawing in Early Renaissance Italy. Yale University Press, 2000.

Gage, John. Color and Culture: Practice and Meaning from Antiquity to Abstraction. University of California Press, 1999.

Gage, John. Color and Meaning: Art, Science and Symbolism. University of California Press, 1999.

Kandinsky, Wassily. Concerning the Spiritual in Art. Translated by M. T. H. Sadler, Dover Publications, 1977.

Malevich, Kazimir. Red Square. 1915, State Russian Museum, St. Petersburg.

Matisse, Henri. Harmony in Red (The Red Room). 1908, Hermitage Museum, St. Petersburg.

Pastoureau, Michel. Red: The History of a Color. Princeton University Press, 2017.

Rothko, Mark. Untitled (Red, Black, Orange). 1960, National Gallery of Art, Washington, D.C.

Taylor, Paul. The Oxford Companion to the History of Modern Science. Oxford University Press, 2003.

Weiwei, Ai. Sunflower Seeds. 2010, Tate Modern, London.

Bassous, Reem. Reem Bassous. reembassous.studio. Accessed 9 Aug. 2025.

Danner, Morgan. "Morgan Danner." Rensselaer Architecture. arch.rpi.edu/2013/05/morgan-danner/. Accessed 9 Aug. 2025.

Dehghan, Mahsa. Portfolio. mahsadehghan.my.canva.site. Accessed 9 Aug. 2025.

Mura, Piet. Piet K. Mura. pietkm6.wixsite.com. Accessed 9 Aug. 2025.

Navarro-MacLochlainn, Pablo. Pablo Navarro-MacLochlainn (Instagram profile). instagram.com/kritios_boi/. Accessed 9 Aug. 2025.

Tesse, Enne. Enne Tesse. ennetesse.wixsite.com. Accessed 9 Aug. 2025.